A Quick Guide from THE REBEL DIVA SERIES

THE FEAR BUSTER

THREE ESSENTIAL DECISION MAKING TOOLS

THREE TOOLS TO CONQUER YOUR FEARS AND MAKE SMARTER DECISIONS AT WORK & IN LIFE.

Tikiri

"You gain strength, courage, and confidence by every experience in which you really stop to look fear in the face. You must do the thing which you think you cannot do."
~ Eleanor Roosevelt

FREE AUDIO DOWNLOAD

Get the shortcut to conquering your fears so you can follow your dreams.
Listen as you go with the audio for this mini book.
You'll find details on how to download your personal copy of the *Bust Your Fears* audio at the end of this book.

I'll see you on the inside!
Tikiri

The Rebel Diva Self-Empowerment Series

This mini book is part of the Rebel Diva books and online program universe.

There are four main books in the Rebel Diva series: (1) *Your Rebel Dreams,* (2) *Your Rebel Plans,* (3) *Your Rebel Life,* and (4) *The Fear Buster.*

The first book, *Your Rebel Dreams,* shares an easy-to-follow process to help you discover your fundamental purpose and passions in life, and identify your innate talents you can harness to make a living doing what you love to do.

The second book, *Your Rebel Plans,* offers a step-by-step, structured system on how to create a master plan for your career success, including how to set smart goals that will get you to your life dreams. This master plan is all about getting you from where you are today to where you want to be in life.

The third book, *Your Rebel Life,* provides easy habit hacks for the ten most important pillars of your life. These habits are designed to get your life in order, from your finances to your career to your relationships, and more.

This book you hold in your hands, *The Fear Buster*, tackles one aspect of the Rebel Diva mindset—and that it how to dance with fear to help you make the tough decisions you need to make, so you can follow your dreams with joy.

Is this you?

Do you dream of quitting your job to follow your passions, but worry you'll crash and end up living under a bridge?

Do you desperately want to change your career but the thought of starting something new breaks you into a sweat?

Do you wish to find work you truly love, maybe start a small business or even go back to school but feel too paralyzed to take that first step?

If you said yes to any of these questions, this book is for you.

Yes, you!

Wherever you're living, whichever type of work you're doing or whatever you dream to do next, I know how you feel. I know because I've been there too—not once, but many times in my past chaotic life.

Busting Our Fears

The Rebel Diva books are all about tackling our fears and making the brave decision to pursue work we love doing—our calling in life, whatever that might be. Life's too short not to follow our dreams. We never want to end up at our deathbeds with the regret of not having done what we desired to do on earth.

But before we can follow our passions, we must conquer the anxieties that live inside us so we can boldly take our first step toward our dreams. We must get into the right mindset to make those life-changing decisions with confidence and competence.

That Sinking Feeling...

Though many of us know deep inside that we're bigger and better than the job we're doing right now, that we'd really like to change our career trajectory, we tend to keep our heads down and carry on with our mundane and unhappy lives because we're too scared to make the shift.

BUST YOUR FEARS: 3 EASY TOOLS TO REDUCE YOUR STRESS & MAKE SMARTER CHOICES FASTER

I'm familiar with that sinking feeling that sits in your gut—that feeling that signals to you that you need to be someplace else, somewhere so much nicer than this. You deliberately ignore that feeling because it's hard to look at truth in the face.

I know what that's like.

I used to get panic attacks on Sunday nights when the thought of walking into a job I hated the next morning crossed my mind. I used to experience that crippling sense of dread that worms into your head in the middle of the night making you toss and turn for hours. I used to wake up every morning groggy and tired, then grit my teeth through the day, trying to convince myself and others that I'm "fine."

It took me a long time to realize I needed to do something about my unhappiness at work. But I was too scared. I got very good at worrying, despairing, over-thinking and over analyzing, all to distract myself from doing the two most important things: making a decision and taking action.

One day, I finally looked in the mirror and had a talk to with myself. I told myself that it was up to me to make the change and the time was now. I reminded myself how foolish it was to be handcuffed by thinking the devil I knew was better than the one I didn't (if one existed at all). And then, I told myself to feel the fear and do it, anyway.

What I Learned

What I did after that was not throw fear to the curb and brazenly jump off a cliff. I learned to pause and think through my fears, acknowledge them, harness them to my advantage and take smart, calculated risks. It was this shift that helped me get to my goals faster. I learned how to pack my parachute so I could make the bodacious decisions I yearned to make and embark on an exciting journey with my eyes wide open.

And what did that bring me?

A life of sanity, serenity, and success. And happiness. Much happiness. I now know the joy of waking up in the morning to do work I love doing. Gone are my headaches, migraines, and stomach upsets. I am left wondering only one thing: why didn't I do this sooner? Why did I wait so long mired with worry before I took my first step toward freedom? Ah, but that's what makes me human, I guess. I've accepted this now and am grateful I learned my lesson and moved onward.

What about you?

Are you ready to tackle your deepest fears and explore a new career, a new job, or an exciting new path in your life? A path that's aligned to who you are, one that will bring you more joy and happiness?

A Fear-Busting Solution

I know it's easy to talk about change or to hear how someone else did it, but it's much harder to curb your own fears and take that first step.

BUST YOUR FEARS: 3 EASY TOOLS TO REDUCE YOUR STRESS & MAKE SMARTER CHOICES FASTER

So, I created three simple fear-busting tools you can apply to the doubts and dilemmas that might be whirling in your brain right now. If you want to reel in your anxieties, get over your fears and tackle the biggest decisions you're facing in your life right now, the tools in this book will show you how.

There are three decision-making tools in here that will take the emotions of anxiety, fear, and worry out of the equation and help you make the career choices you want to make (or any life decision for that matter) with clarity and confidence.

The concepts here are based on industry best standards and practices but have been simplified and personalized so anyone can use them for everyday situations. They can assist you whether you need to summon your courage to talk to your boss about a promotion, decide whether to take a year off work and travel the world or to embark on a whole new career path.

Large corporations and organizations use complex risk management models to successfully make multimillion-dollar decisions. The philosophy is the same, but the tools here are more foundational and easy to use. All you need is fifteen minutes of quiet me-time and a pen and paper. And an open mind of course.

This is calculated risk management for the rest of us.

The Five Aspects of Fear
False Evidence Appearing Real

First, let's dissect this thing called fear. Once we do this, a world of possibilities will open to us.

So, where does fear come from?

Fear is how you and I react to an incident or a person we believe will harm us.

It's a learned behavior we picked up from a young age watching how our parents, siblings or teachers responded to different situations, people and events.

So, if we can learn fear, then surely we can unlearn it, can't we?

But before we go about discovering how to unlearn what we learned and manage our fears better, let's unravel this thing we call fear and look at it through a more objective lens. Here are five important aspects of fear so we can understand it better and harness it, so it works for us rather than against us.

1. Fear Is Advantageous

The ancient part of our brain, the amygdala, is responsible for processing fear and has done a great job of it for millennia. It was fear that helped our ancestors avoid getting mauled by a saber-toothed tiger. It was fear that got them ready to fight that nasty big cat or flee from it and get themselves to safety. Note that tiger is now extinct while we humans are still here—in the billions and counting.

So, fear is a useful emotion and serves a purpose.

For example, it's perfectly reasonable, and probably an extremely smart thing to be fearful of someone running down the street screaming with a bloodied knife in their hands. The emotions that arise when you witness such a sight will allow you to react quickly and take the necessary precautions to get yourself to safety. Or defend yourself if need be.

Now, most of us are fortunate to live in modern environments in relatively safe neighborhoods where the chances of coming across a crazed maniac like that are pretty slim. Not to say this doesn't happen. You just have to watch the nightly news to find out. But for most of us, the probability of seeing this is quite low.

Fear has an essential part to play in our lives. The problem is our crocodile brains haven't caught up to our contemporary lifestyles yet.

Think of fear as an important signal that's telling you something you need to know. If you're feeling anxious walking into a job interview or into a bank to ask for a business loan, that just means this is important to you. It means you're about to stretch yourself and take a leap forward.

Acknowledge your feelings. Embrace them. Then, ask yourself if you have any unanswered questions you need to explore before you take that step. Putting your mind into problem-solving mode is an excellent way to move forward, instead of mulling over your anxieties.

"Don't be afraid of your fears. They're not there to scare you. They're there to let you know that something is worth it."

C. JoyBell C.

---

2. Fear Is Disadvantageous

Our minds trigger fear whenever they believe there's a threat on the horizon. And today, these fearful emotions arise in the most mundane (if you really think about it) of circumstances.

Your throat may dry up and you may start sweating as you walk into a job interview. You may get butterflies in your stomach and feel a tremble in your knees as you get up to give a talk in public. You may get clammy palms just thinking about asking for a promotion at work.

None of these circumstances is life-threatening. But our brains don't know the difference and flood our bodies with stress hormones, preparing ourselves to fight or flee as if there's a mean-looking saber-toothed tiger hiding behind the coffee table in the office boardroom.

Some stress is beneficial. It heightens our awareness, gets us excited and pushes us forward to do what we're about to engage in. And that is a good thing. A great thing.

The problem arises when we focus on the worst possible outcomes and allow our fears to overtake our minds. That's when we either stop or delay taking the action we know we must take.

This might mean we never ask for that promotion and sit back to grudgingly watch Jack get the job instead. It might mean we say no to speaking engagements that would have helped our career or our business. We might remain in unhappy jobs simply because we're too scared to venture into the unknown.

Fear has got us then. And our lives become much worse for it.

Take ten quiet minutes for yourself and ask yourself if the emotions you're feeling have a solid basis. Look for evidence for your worries. Then, instead of focusing on the worst-case scenario, focus on your best-case one. You might just discover that what you're feeling is only a knee jerk reaction that will hinder your progress than help you move forward.

BUST YOUR FEARS: 3 EASY TOOLS TO REDUCE YOUR STRESS & MAKE SMARTER CHOICES FASTER

"A great deal of fear is a result of just not knowing. We do not know what is involved in a new situation. We do not know whether we can deal with it. The sooner we learn what it entails, the sooner we can dissolve our fear."
— Eleanor Roosevelt

3. The Future Is Uncertain

If there's one thing we can be certain of in life, it's uncertainty.

Nothing is guaranteed and no one has a crystal ball to predict the future.

So, we never know how that chat with the boss would have turned out or how our performance during that talk might have panned out. There is always an element of risk in everything we do.

If we truly desire to be a hundred percent fear-free, we might as well call it a day, lock the doors and sleep under our beds for the rest of our lives. But that's not what I'd call living.

What we fail to realize is even if our manager says "no" to our request for a promotion, we might learn something important during that conversation. Maybe that nugget of information will help you to snag the job next year. Or you may get a signal that it's time to move on elsewhere, which is also a positive outcome. Otherwise, you'd have languished in that job hoping, wishing, praying for someone to notice you, all the while getting disgruntled and miserable.

That uncertainty of not knowing how things will turn out accentuates our fear and keeps us from taking action, even when it can help us.

What we need to come to terms with—as much as we'd rather not—is that dealing with uncertainty is part of the human journey. It's by wading through our problems and challenges and issues that we grow and strengthen. We shouldn't be actively avoiding fear, but walking toward it bravely, ready to tackle it head-on.

I understand that this might be hard to swallow, especially if you're going through a particularly rough patch at the moment. You may feel like yelling out, "I don't need to grow anymore, for heaven's sake!" But that leaves you open to even more risks, because ignoring your problems and not tackling your issues directly only makes them multiply.

> "Our fear of the unknown and our fear of making mistakes trick us into focusing on what we don't know or can't do. When we give ourselves the freedom to be uncertain and less than perfect, then we can start thinking, 'What do I know? What can I do?' That's when the adventure starts—learning, thriving, conquering, failing, recouping, and having a ton of fun."
>
> Kristin Smith

4. Uncertainty Is Neutral

The future can hold either negative possibilities or positive possibilities. We all know this.

If you have goals and a desire to move forward, whether it's to interview for a job in a new field, apply for a college degree as a mature student, or pitch a new business idea for funds, you must be willing to keep an open mind.

To become successful in any area of your life, you'll need to learn to make decisions without having all the cards in your hands. You'll need to embrace ambiguity.

If we wait for all the correct answers, the perfect plans and acknowledgment from everyone around us before we take action, we'll remain stuck forever. And that is the greatest risk of them all. Not making a decision out of fear of what the future might bring means we're opening ourselves to whatever life throws our way. And that is not a good place to get stuck.

Those worst-case scenarios that whirl through our brains when we are overcome by fear rarely manifest themselves. Mark Twain once famously said, "I am an old man and have known a great many troubles, but most of them never happened." How true.

So let's take control of our lives and careers. It's when we start moving forward regardless of our fears that we can stay alert, change direction to avoid bumps and proactively focus on where we want to go.

If we want to make the bold and brave career choices we know we deserve, we must become comfortable with being uncomfortable.

That's right. Give ambiguity a big hug and a kiss—that's how close you'll need to get to it.

We want to be victors at life, not victims of it.

> *"Fear, to a great extent, is born of a story we tell ourselves, and so I chose to tell myself a different story from the one women are told. I decided I was safe. I was strong. I was brave. Nothing could vanquish me. Insisting on this story was a form of mind control, but for the most part, it worked."*
>
> Cheryl Strayed

5. You Can Prepare for Risks

Obstacles are a fact of life. And they are not always an indication of the quality of your personal goals, your plans, or your actions.

The best way to prepare for obstacles that may crop up in your life—and they will—is to anticipate them in advance and consider how you can best address them.

When you're mentally prepared for future risks and have a general idea of how to respond, you'll find yourself in a powerful position where few things unsettle you. You'll feel more balanced and ready to face any problems on your route, even those you haven't anticipated yet.

On the other hand, if you ignore potential risks altogether, that may open you up to nasty surprises in the future. And if you're not ready to face these issues along the way, you may want to retreat at the first sight of a problem.

In the same vein, you cannot and should not—ever—sit around trying to think of all the potential risks in your life. That will get you stuck

BUST YOUR FEARS: 3 EASY TOOLS TO REDUCE YOUR STRESS & MAKE SMARTER CHOICES FASTER

in analysis paralysis. And that is a surefire path to getting immobilized with fear.

The trick to managing our fears is to keep our eyes wide open, be prepared for potential obstacles but stay positive and plow through with what we need and want to do to get to the other side.

The tools in this guidebook are designed to do just that. They will help you assess your risks as objectively as possible so you can make smart career decisions faster.

Four Mindset Shifts

"Write down everything you fear in life. Burn it.
Pour herbal oil with a sweet scent on the ashes."
Yoko Ono

Before we get to the fear-busting decision-making tools, let's look at four essential mindset shifts you need to have. These shifts will enhance your capacity to manage your fears as you go on your career-change journey.

1. Know Your Values

One of the most compelling ways to manage your fears is to ask how the question or issue you're facing is linked to your fundamental values. If you have a strong enough *why*, you'll see the answers clearly in front of you and most dilemmas will easily resolve themselves.

Your purpose becomes the compass that will guide you.

Self-awareness is one of the most powerful weapons you can carry with you when you face the uncertainties of life. When you know who you are and what you want, you increase your capacity to fight back fear in the face of the unknown.

For example, if one of your fundamental values is respect, it will propel you to treat others with as much respect as you expect them to treat you. You won't tolerate bad behavior and you will, through your actions and words, show others where you draw the line. This means the probability you'll fall into a bad work environment in the first place, a situation where you're crippled with fear because of how someone treated you, becomes quite low. And if you do come across such circumstances, you'll know exactly what to do.

But not all of us have a strong indication of our personal values. This is why our fears and problems become insurmountable in the first place.

Finding your values will take introspection and self-awareness and won't happen overnight. If you're looking for a structured process to figure your values out, the first book of the Rebel Diva series, *Your Rebel Dreams*, is designed to do just that. In the meantime, the tools in this booklet will help you get over any fear that will hold you back from taking the right actions so you can get on with your life.

2. Trust Your Instincts

But what about our instincts? I can hear you say. *Shouldn't we pay attention to them?*

Absolutely. And without question. Our gut is even considered a "second brain" and can comprehend situations faster than that complex organ in our head can most times.

But when you're at a point of indecision because of anxiety and stress, you're probably not in the right frame of mind (or body) to depend on your gut. To go with your instincts, you must be in tune with yourself and able to listen to your body carefully. Usually, when we're in a state of fear and worry, we're not listening to our logical brain let alone the subtle hints the rest of our body is sending us.

My recommendation is to take stock of your situation rationally using the tools here. Just going through the thinking process will calm you down and get you to a point where you're able to think more clearly and listen to other signals.

Once you're done with the analytical thinking, ask yourself if there are any red flags you're getting from your gut. Consider them seriously, together with the logical answers you've come up with before making your final decision.

Never ignore your instincts but know when it's the right time to rely on them.

3. Seek Gratitude

When we're feeling afraid or anxious, we tend to ruminate about the worst that can happen and even feel sorry for ourselves. Can you relate? I know I can.

But if we get mired in these unhelpful thoughts, we can fall down a deep spiral of negativity that will be hard to get out of.

One of the best ways to avoid drowning in fear is to take a pause. Take a deep breath in and out, then ask yourself what you have to be grateful about right now. You see, gratitude is a powerful emotion, so powerful that it can't exist in our heads together with a negative thought. By fostering gratitude, you will banish the fears and worries rumbling through your mind.

If you're reading this, your standard of living (shelter, food, clothing, safety, education, work opportunities, freedom of expression and movement etc... etc...) is miles ahead of 90 percent of the world's population. If we truly look around us, we have little to complain about. It's a travesty if we do, really. To even consider changing your career and following your passions is a privilege many around the planet do not have.

The opportunities in front of us are endless if we only open our eyes to look. How can we not feel thankful for this?

As Albert Einstein once said, "There are only two ways to live your life. One is as though nothing is a miracle. The other is as though everything is a miracle."

With an attitude of gratitude like that, how can fear even sneak in?

4. Be a Bison Not a Cow

I want to share with you a story that comes from the wide plains of North America—a story about bison and cows. Yes, you read that right. There is an important lesson we can learn from how our bovine friends react to storms.

Whenever a thunderstorm brews on the horizon, cow herds usually turn tail and run in the opposite direction.

Unfortunately, cows (or humans for that matter) can never outrun a storm and so get caught up in it quickly, getting drenched to the bone. They also stay in the squall for longer because they are now traveling in the same direction as the storm!

On the other hand, the much smarter bison herds face the storm and wait for it to approach them. Then, when it gets really close, they charge right through it with determination. This way, they minimize the impact and get through the storm to the other side faster.

This is a great metaphor for how we, humans, can deal with the chaos and conflicts of life. If we procrastinate on dealing with our issues, ignore our problems or try to run away from them, we'll only get entrenched in the pain for longer.

The smartest and healthiest thing you can do is to face your fears. Even one small step to tackling the issue will take you closer to getting you out of the tempest. Then, take another small step. And another. This will help you get out sooner and also make you better prepared to face the next storm life rains on you.

Strive to become like the mighty bison. Not the cowardly cow.

> *"Cows run away from the storm while the buffalo charges toward it—and gets through it quicker. Whenever I'm confronted with a tough challenge, I do not prolong the torment, I become the buffalo."*
>
> Wilma Mankiller, the first female chief of the Cherokee nation

BUST YOUR FEARS: 3 EASY TOOLS TO REDUCE YOUR STRESS & MAKE SMARTER CHOICES FASTER

"Everything is figuroutable."
~ Marie Forleo

Three Easy Fear-Busting Tools

"Nothing in life is to be feared, it is only to be understood. Now is the time to understand more, so that we may fear less."

Marie Curie

Okay, let's move on to the fear-busting tools. The three decision-making tools in this booklet are:

1. The Fear Matrix
2. The Fear Buster
3. The Lemonade Maker

These tools are simplified versions of more complex, best-in-industry models I've used in the corporate world for more than a decade to assess risks in large-scale programs. I recently realized how they can help us solve everyday personal problems just as easily as they can multi-million dollar business ones.

If you really think about it, there is nothing rocket-science-cy about these tools I am about to show you. They are simple ideas based on common sense. All they do is lift the fog of fear from your brain, when it's most difficult to, and force you to see the problem clearly and come to conclusions you otherwise might not have.

As the world-renown author, Brendon Burchard often likes to say, "common sense is not always common practice." This is one reason we fall into sticky holes and find it hard to get out. These tools will help you gear up on common sense and put it into practice so the solutions you come up with will make logical sense to you and others.

How These Tools Work

These three tools will show you how to view the uncertainties in your life, especially as you embark on a bold career change or switch in jobs, in a more rational manner than your ancient amygdala is capable of. They can remove your biases, present you with a more objective view of the world, and increase the accuracy with which you look at problems and their consequences.

They'll help you take control over your emotions and let the modern part of your brain run the show, so you can be prepared to meet your future head-on with eyes wide open.

These tools have now become an important arsenal in my own personal development toolbox. They have helped me, time and time again, to make difficult decisions, deal with conflicts more rationally, get over debilitating stupor, and take action when I thought I never could.

All you need is a pen and a paper and fifteen quiet minutes to jot down the answers to the questions in these tools.

If you don't have the time or if you're not a fan of writing things out (though writing helps to retain information and clarify your thoughts and so is highly recommended), you can go through these exercises mentally and let your mind come up with quick answers.

There are examples provided for each tool, so you can see how they work.

Good luck!

A Few Things to Remember

There will always be an element of human subjectivity when using any problem-solving tool. All of this will depend on your perspective, viewpoint, and life experiences.

While these tools bring about more objectivity, you will not find the exact "right answers." In fact, there are no right answers to anything in life. So, use these tools like you would a GPS to guide you on your route but ultimately, you must make your own choices.

One way to mitigate your subjectivity is to do these exercises with a trusted friend. Brainstorming with someone who knows you well and has your best interests at heart may help you get through these questions faster and also make you feel like someone's standing in your corner.

This alone can reduce those feelings of anxiety so you can make the decisions you need to make with a clear mind.

If you'd like the larger sized, printable tables in this book, you can download the worksheets at BookHip.com/JWTNJH[1]

---

1. https://bookhip.com/JWTNJH

Fear-Busting Tool #1: The Fear Matrix

The Fear Matrix
The main goal of this tool is to put our fears into perspective.

If you're grappling with several issues simultaneously, this tool will put them on a risk matrix so you can get a clearer vision of which are the most significant and which are the least.

This way, you won't run around trying to tackle all your problems, getting overwhelmed and drained. You can prioritize your issues and manage the biggest headaches first. Then, you can take care of the smaller ones when you're feeling less pressure.

If you're on the verge of a career transition, you may be grappling a few things at work and probably at home too, on top of the stress of a potential change. Here are some examples of fears that went coursing through my head during my last career transition. If you have a family and especially young children, you may very well double or triple this list!

- "I don't enjoy my job any more. I spend way too much time at work and my office feels like a torture chamber. They'll all find out how much I hate it and fire me. I just know it."
- "Ugh. I can't stand my new boss. He's creepy. The last time he invited me to his office, he tried to get way too close."
- "My department head "voluntold" me to speak at the next work seminar, but I don't have time to prepare. I'm going to embarrass myself in front of everyone."
- "Finally snagged a job interview with this amazing company next Monday, but I'm so stressed, I feel like I won't do a good job. What if they reject me? I'll never get out of *this* job."
- "I promised my sick friend I'd visit her last weekend, but I was working as usual. I have to see her on Saturday and take flowers. Lots of

flowers and soup. Hope she doesn't hate me. Oh my god, she must think I'm a horrible person."

- "Eeek. There's a wasp nest in the garage!! What if they come into the house?"
- "I feel like I'm failing in everything life and will end up living under a bridge...."
- And there was more....

Imagine having to deal with all this and kids, if you have kids. It's enough to make you go insane. I nearly did. And if you really think about it, most of these don't require hitting the panic button, even though you may feel like it in the moment.

Now you may have an amazing disposition where you can handle several stressful events all at once and still come out like a Mother Teresa. But I certainly didn't. I stressed and worried and ruminated. I gnashed my teeth, ate badly, slept badly, got sick often, and found myself on the borderline of a temper tantrum at any time of the day.

It was a miserable existence. My relationships suffered. And it was not helping me solve my problems or get closer to my goal of transitioning to a better job.

One Friday evening, I decided enough was enough, that I had to *do* something.

But all I could think of was to sit with a pen and paper and write down all the things that were happening in my life, all those things that inflamed the fight, flight or freeze response in me.

Then, I re-arranged my list from "that's the worst thing that's happened in my life, ever," to "yup, that's kinda bad."

At that time, I was using a complex risk management tool to manage my large-scale projects at work. Looking down at my personal list, I wondered if I could simplify this tool and apply it to the personal issues I was facing in my life.

And I could!

BUST YOUR FEARS: 3 EASY TOOLS TO REDUCE YOUR STRESS & MAKE SMARTER CHOICES FASTER

I drew up a much simpler risk matrix using just two criteria to prioritize my problems and get a better perspective of my fears.

These two criteria are:

1. What's the probability the worst-case scenario will happen here?
2. How bad is this worst-case scenario?

Using these two criteria, I plotted my issues on my brand new simplified Fear Matrix.

Once I saw all my problems in relation to each other, I knew where to focus my attention first. I could also come up with logical solutions to tackle each of the problems, starting with the most important and urgent one first and moving on to the less urgent and important ones.

As I thought through the problems on my plate and plotted them on the matrix, I discovered an amazing side benefit as well. My stress levels went down dramatically. I managed to wrestle down the incessant internal voice that was throwing red flags all over the place and ratcheting up the fear factor. I started to breathe again and think clearly again.

Let's look at two examples so you can understand how this tool works.

The Fear Matrix - Example One

Here's the Fear Matrix I completed using the issues I listed previously—the ones I was grappling with during that tough job search week.

As you can see, some of the problems I feared the most, those I thought would bring the end-of-the-world, were really not as bad as I feared and were eventually solvable.

You know that totally unsubstantiated fear that had snuck into the back of my brain, the one where I was sure my career was over and I'd end up living under a bridge? As I tried to figure out where this would fit in the matrix, I realized it had a low, almost zero probability of happening even though the result would be disastrous. After realizing this, I knew not to fill my mind with this useless worry.

From all my problems that week, having a colony of wasps in the garage was the most pressing (and dangerous) issue. This was what I had to tackle most urgently. But since I'd been ruminating over all my other problems, it had slipped my mind and had become secondary, until I took the time to see everything in perspective.

Ironically, even if the other work-related problems materialized as-is, I realized after doing this exercise that things were not that bad. And here was my A-Ha moment: it's those scenarios we believe will break us that actually help us see our life path more clearly and push us to make the changes we truly need to make.

BUST YOUR FEARS: 3 EASY TOOLS TO REDUCE YOUR STRESS & MAKE SMARTER CHOICES FASTER

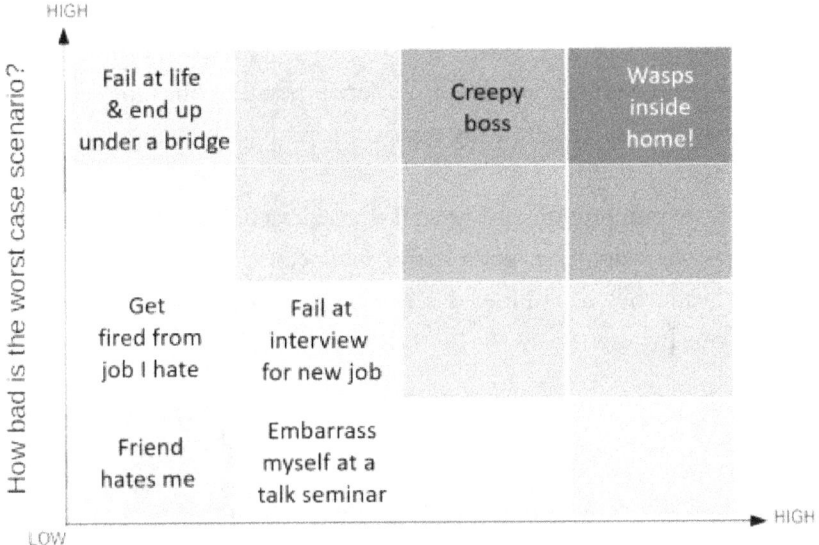

Keep in mind that everyone's personal priorities and preferences are different. Your answers to the two questions on this matrix may differ depending on your age, your experiences, your opinions, and other life circumstances.

Your matrix should tell your story. Use these examples as guidance on how to use the matrix but remember to tell your own story.

The Fear Matrix - Example Two

Here's a second example of the Fear Matrix from a colleague who was dealing with a difficult parenting issue on top of a job change and some work issues.

She was wrangling quite a few fear-based scenarios. Putting all this down on paper helped her get a better perspective of her problems and eased her headaches. This allowed her to create a game plan to tackle each problem, one by one.

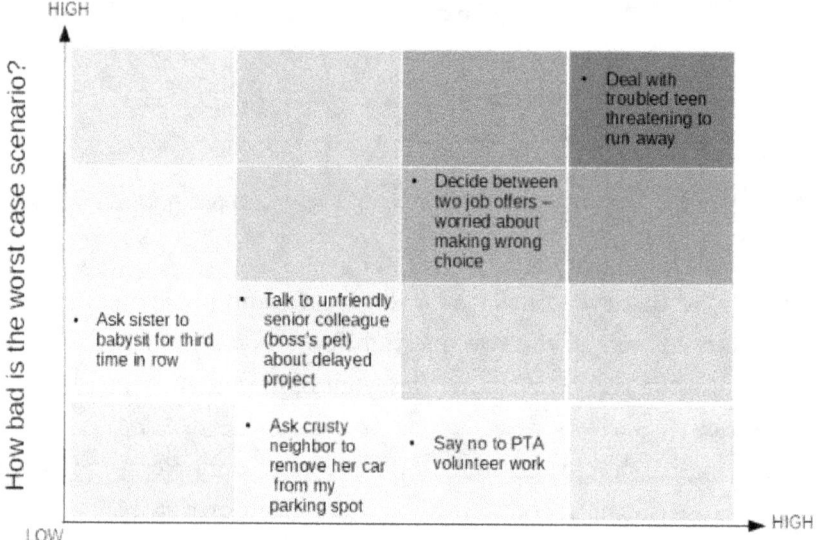

BUST YOUR FEARS: 3 EASY TOOLS TO REDUCE YOUR STRESS & MAKE SMARTER CHOICES FASTER

Your Turn

Use the Fear Matrix to jot down all your problems so you can view them with respect to each other.

Imagine you're flying in a small plane over a landscape made up of your life right now, seeing all your fears laid down below in relation to each other. This matrix will give you the 50,000-foot level view.

If you're having trouble with this exercise, ask yourself these two questions for each fear-inducing problem:

- Will this issue matter six months from now?
- Will this issue matter two years from now?

Here's Your First Step

List the problems you're facing right now—those that instill some form of fear or anxiety in you.

The simple act of writing your problems down will help you see it in clearer light, so take a journal or the print copy of this book. Then, jot down your issues on the Fear Matrix in relation to each other. An unfilled matrix is shared on the next page for you to print out and use.

Your Question:

The things in my life that are troubling me right now:

Issue #1:
_____

Issue #2:
_____

Issue #3:
_____

Issue #4: _____

Issue #5: _____

The Fear Matrix

Scrutinize the five (or more) issues you wrote just now and see if you can slot them into this matrix by answering the two questions below.

For each of your issues, ask yourself:

1. What's the probability the worst-case scenario will happen?
2. How bad is the worst-case scenario, really?

Now fit it into the most relevant square. This will be eye-opening if you hadn't taken the time to think through it all before.

"Courage is the most important of all the virtues, because without courage you can't practice any other virtue consistently. You can practice any virtue erratically, but nothing consistently without courage."
~Maya Angelou

Fear-Busting Tool #2: The Fear Buster

The Fear Buster

The Fear Buster takes one problem you have and forces you to look at it from all sides, searching for evidence of your fears. When you go through this exercise, you'll find that what you fear the most may be insignificant or not even exist, most of the time.

The questions you will ask yourself here are:

The Worst-Case Scenario:

- What am I expecting to go wrong?

- What assumptions am I making, and how true are they?

- What steps can I take to reduce this worst-case scenario into a more manageable one?

The Best-Case Scenario:

- What am I expecting to go spectacularly right?

- What assumptions am I making, and how true are they?

- What steps can I take to increase the chances of this best-case scenario happening?

Since our human brains are naturally wired to mull over negative possibilities, we only think of worst-case scenarios that can heighten anxiety and stifle action. After this exercise, you may find those scenarios diminish and positive options you may never have contemplated show up.

The Fear Buster tool will force you to look at all sides of the picture and ask questions you may not have considered before. This will help calm your anxieties and find out-of-the-box solutions before jumping to conclusions, or worse, taking action that could backfire on you later on.

Our Fears

You can apply this tool to any difficult situation that's filling you with dread or to a decision you're hesitating to make because of the many unknowns surrounding it.

Here are some common work-related fears you can dissect within minutes using the Fear Buster tool.

Have any of these thoughts crept into your mind recently?

- "I just finished an important project that got rave reviews from our clients. But I don't think I get paid enough for all the hard work I do. Some days, I feel like I'm underpaid. I've got to talk to my boss about this but am worried about approaching her. What if she says no? What if I get blacklisted for asking for more?"
- "I feel like everyone's getting ahead in this company except for me. I'm constantly overlooked for promotions and one reason is because I don't have a degree. I'm sure of it. So, should I go to college? How will I find the time? Can I even afford it? Could I ask my company to pay?"
- "I just told my team I'm pregnant. They were all nice about it, but some of them are already preparing for my departure and creeping on my projects. My boss congratulated me, but I could see the unease in his eyes, like he thought I was going to be a burden. I'm not dying for heaven's sake, just pregnant! I'm worried they'll push me aside. Did I just cut myself off the promotion ladder?"
- "I'm not happy at work anymore. The environment is negative, the work is boring and I don't find my projects fun and stimulating like they used to. I don't know what I want to do next, but I know this is not it. What if I take a year off to think through all this? But will a sabbatical kill my career? How will that time off look on my resume?" (Remember this situation as we will use it as an example on this tool.)

BUST YOUR FEARS: 3 EASY TOOLS TO REDUCE YOUR STRESS & MAKE SMARTER CHOICES FASTER 37

You can run any of these fears through the Fear Buster tool to gain more perspective and seek better solutions, but this doesn't mean you can glibly ignore your instincts.

Your gut is almost always right. Perhaps your unethical boss and team are truly uneasy about your pregnancy and are not open to maternity leave. If that's the case, going through this exercise will help you respond to the situation with more information and ammunition on your side.

It will help you come up with solutions that take the other party's views into consideration. This will make it harder for them to shut you down quickly. They will be forced to listen at least.

Do this exercise to think through your problems rationally and then see how your gut feels about it. Together, they form a powerful weapon in your toolbox.

*If you'd like the larger sized, printable tables in this book, you can download the worksheets at BookHip.com/JWTNJH[1]

---

1. https://bookhip.com/JWTNJH

The Fear Buster - Example One

This example takes one of the fears listed earlier and dissects it further.

Most of the time, the solutions you come up with in the last columns of both the best and worst-case scenarios can be very similar. Sometimes, they are identical, just like here. That's because sometimes whichever way you look at the problem, the resolutions are more or less the same.

Upcoming Decision I'm Worrying About:

"I'm not happy at work anymore. The environment is negative, the work is boring and I don't find my projects fun and stimulating like they used to. I don't know what I want to do next but I know this is not it. What if I can take a year off, a sabbatical to think through all this? But will a sabbatical kill my career? Will it look bad on my resume? I'm worried taking time off will leave a black mark on my CV."

WORST-CASE SCENARIO			BEST-CASE SCENARIO		
What am I expecting to go wrong?	What assumptions am I making here, and how true are they?	What steps can I take to reduce this scenario into a more manageable one?	What can go spectacularly right?	What assumptions am I making here, and how true are they?	What steps can I take to increase the chances of this scenario happening?
- Spouse may not be too happy. - Loss of income. - All my savings get siphoned off. - Lose my job / position at work. - Get cut off from future promotions. - Leave a black mark on my CV. - Slow down my career progress. - Return culture shock.	- That my spouse may not understand how unhappy I am at work. - That my boss and team would look at my sabbatical in a negative light. - That future employers will look at sabbatical in a negative light. - That I won't be able to manage my finances and have to cut leave short. *None are 100% accurate and need to be explored	- Talk to spouse and show how this can help family get closer. - Make a financial plan and save up before taking leave. - Talk to boss about preparing for return before leaving. - Talk to others who've done this successfully and get tips. - Make new connections on my sabbatical to explore new jobs or career ideas.	- Peace of mind from getting away from negative work environment. - Travel and visit places on my bucket list. - Get healthy again. - Have time with kids and spouse again. - Opportunity to explore or find a new career. - Come back refreshed and energized.	- That I can prepare for my leave in a smart way. - That my family will see the benefits of this idea for all. - That I can make this work and use it to explore new paths and maybe even a new career. - That after this, I may not have to come back to the same work environment. *If I put my mind to this, this is do-able!	- Talk to spouse and show how this can help family get closer. - Make a financial plan and save up before taking leave. - Talk to boss about preparing for return before leaving. - Talk to others who've done this successfully and get tips. - Make new connections on my sabbatical to explore new jobs or career ideas.

The Fear Buster - Example Two

Here's an example of the Fear Buster from a colleague who was dealing with a difficult issue at work to give you another perspective of how this can work.

Upcoming Conversation I'm Fearing at Work:
"Talk to boss about an unfriendly, senior colleague who's delaying a project. I'm worried the project's poor performance is going to be blamed on me. I feel like my colleague is jeopardizing the project and my career prospects in this company."

WORST-CASE SCENARIO			BEST-CASE SCENARIO		
What am I expecting to go wrong?	What assumptions am I making here, and how true are they?	What steps can I take to reduce this scenario into a more manageable one?	What can go spectacularly right?	What assumptions am I making here, and how true are they?	What steps can I take to increase the chances of this scenario happening?
- Colleague will delay project and screw up my deadlines. - This will reflect badly on me and I may lose my performance bonus. - My boss won't be too happy with me and I may not be considered for the next promotion or pay raise.	- She hates me! She's is out to get me & has a vendetta against me. - Colleague is not professional and has a bad attitude. - She has issues at home and I wonder if she's taking out her pain at work — and that just happens to be me right now.	- Invite her for a coffee chat. - Explain the importance of the project's deadlines. - Approach her as a team member trying to solve the problem together. - Show her how the project's success will both of us. - Focus on the project, not the person or the personality. - Look for ways to work together.	- She'll work together with me and get the job done right and on time. - The project is a success. - My boss is happy. - My reputation is intact if not better. - I am in line for the next pay raise and promotion.	- She may be dealing with her family issues and doesn't even realizing the harm she's causing the project. - She may not feel like she's part of the team and so isn't communicating to me the work she's done already. Maybe we're more ahead that I think.	- Invite her for a coffee chat. - Explain the importance of the project's deadlines. - Approach her as a team member trying to solve the problem together. - Show her how the project's success will both of us. - Focus on the project, not the person or the personality. - Look for ways to work together.

BUST YOUR FEARS: 3 EASY TOOLS TO REDUCE YOUR STRESS & MAKE SMARTER CHOICES FASTER

Your Turn

Think of one dilemma you're facing right now, the one that makes your stomach constrict every time it crosses your mind.

The simple act of writing a problem down will help you see it in a clearer light, so take a journal or write it in the print copy of this book.

Here's Your First Step

The problem that makes me break into a sweat every time I think about it is:

_____

Now see if you can plug your answers to the Fear Buster questions in the table in the next page.

Seeing your answers on both sides of the table will give excellent clarity to the problem and to your potential solutions and next steps.

The Fear Buster

Fill in the blanks and answer all the questions here. Put down the answers that first pop into your head as they are usually the most accurate.

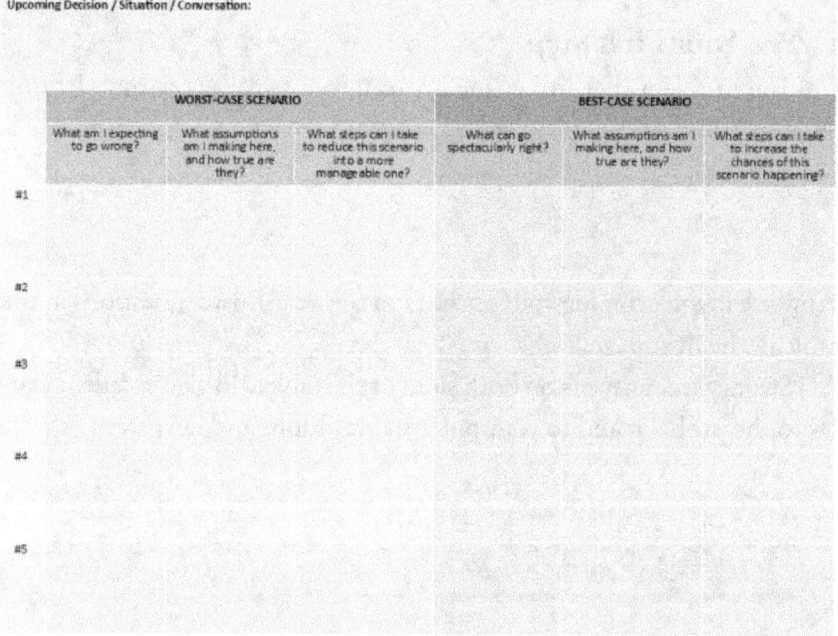

BUST YOUR FEARS: 3 EASY TOOLS TO REDUCE YOUR STRESS & MAKE SMARTER CHOICES FASTER

"When I dare to be powerful, to use my strength in the service of my vision, then it becomes less and less important whether I am afraid."
~ Audre Lorde

Fear-Busting Tool #3: The Lemonade Maker

The Lemonade Maker

Use the Lemonade Maker for those significant issues in life you simply can't shake off or find solutions easily. These are the dreaded decisions that give you nightmares and won't let you sleep for months on end. These are the problems that even the Fear Buster or the Fear Matrix may not have clarified for you.

I believe there is a silver lining in every dark cloud, however black that cloud may be. Even when things are at their harshest, I know deep inside there's a small blessing in disguise if I look hard enough.

Most times, these small nuggets of goodness can turn into amazing life lessons that push you in new directions. They may even bring a whole set of rewards you never imagined before. You just have to dig a bit deep to find them.

Use this tool to seek these rare nuggets out.

So what are some examples that fall into this more extreme fear category?

Adversity at Work

Work-related examples could include:
- Getting fired.
- A layoff or downsizing.
- Sudden demotion at work.
- Bankruptcy.

Adversity in Life

BUST YOUR FEARS: 3 EASY TOOLS TO REDUCE YOUR STRESS & MAKE SMARTER CHOICES FASTER

Bad personal circumstances can hit us when we least expect, and these will impact our work life as well. It's impossible to cleanly separate work and life especially when you're grappling with highly challenging situations at home.

Here's a short list of what I would consider to be personal problems high on the Richter scale. Keep in mind, the perception of what adversity in life is will be different for everyone.

- A chronic illness, like cancer or stroke, in yourself or in a loved one.
- A sudden accident which disables you for the long-term.
- The death of a loved one.
- A traumatic event involving shock or violence.
- A forced move to another country or region.
- Divorce or a difficult separation.

The tool you're about to see will not solve these issues or make them vanish, but they can help you get through these problems by managing your stresses and worries.

As you go through this exercise, remind yourself that there are many brave people in this world who have gone through these situations (or worse) and have overcome them. You're certainly not alone. And these situations are not insurmountable.

---

*If you'd like the larger sized, printable tables in this book, you can download the worksheets at BookHip.com/JWTNJH[1]

---

1. https://bookhip.com/JWTNJH

The Lemonade Maker - Example One

I'd like to share a work-related example from my life—which I felt, at that time, I could never recover from.

Here's what I jotted down one sleepless night to help me understand my situation better and cope with it more intelligently, rather than wallowing in depression or wailing about it day in and day out.

This helped me to stop fighting my circumstances and instead seek opportunities that would make the situation better. Just doing this exercise was a huge stress reliever.

Situation	News of my department downsizing and letting go of a large number of employees, including potentially my team. This is happening in the middle of a recession.
What's keeping me up at night?	The thought I'd lose my job spirals me into a dark place. Worst case scenarios keep playing out in my head. I'm scared I won't be able to pay my mortgage and other necessities. I worry I won't be able to give my family what they need. I feel stressed at the thought of having to find another job in a short period.
Is there a silver lining here?	• Until now, I've complained about my work every single day to anyone who'd listen. Working in this job has made me into a negative, miserable person at home and at work for the past few years. • Now that I may lose it, ironically, I find myself wanting it. But I want it for all the wrong reasons. Do I really want to stay stuck in this place? • If I never got this kick in the pants, I may remain in a miserable job for the rest of my working days. And what a life would that be? • Maybe it's time to let go of this one thing that sucks a huge amount of my time and energy every week and brings me nothing but stress and headaches. • Change is scary, but maybe this is the kick I needed to change my career and do something I love.
What can I do to turn this scenario around?	• Acknowledge that this change is inevitable and use it to my advantage. Know that I'm not alone. Many others have gone through job losses and thrived. They have transformed themselves and followed their dreams. This mind shift alone can lower my stress levels. • Start preparing for change now, so if I'm let go, I'm ready with a plan. Talk to boss about using part of my work day to research jobs. She's affected by this too so she may understand. Doesn't hurt to ask. • Make an inventory of my skills, experience and credentials so I can start looking at what other jobs are out there – jobs I'll actually enjoy doing. • Tap into my contacts across the country, starting now. Even though there's a recession, some cities and some sectors are doing better than others. This is a good time to see what other opportunities there might be. • Talk to my family about my plans and get their support. Show them how this change can help improve our overall standard of living down the road.

Lemonade Maker - Example Two

Here's a more personal example from my life.

Let's be clear though. Plugging your biggest life challenge through this tool doesn't mean it will get resolved magically. You will get a better understanding of where you sit, what's significant, what's not, where you need to focus on and where you shouldn't waste time and energy.

This clarity will help you get through the problem. And that's a much healthier place to be than drowning in despair.

Situation	Receiving a call from the hospital to redo a mammography as they had discovered a lump. Call received a month after relocating to new city.
What's keeping me up at night?	The thought that I've got breast cancer and have to tackle it alone in a new city with no family or friends for support.
Is there a silver lining here?	• Until now, I've not considered my health a priority. This is an opportunity to re-look at my habits, build healthy ones, and re-establish health as my number one priority. • Until now, I've been very critical of my physical appearance so this is a chance to learn to appreciate and love my body as it is. • I've spent the past many years focusing on my career that brought me no fulfillment. This is a wake-up call for me to refocus my attention on the more important things in life. • If I'm going to have to fight this cancer, I'm going to learn to become a true warrior. This means not thinking of myself as a victim or feeling sorry for myself, but fighting back with all I've got and doing everything I can to achieve a healthy life. • This is an opportunity for me to engage with others in the same situation as me, and find ways to make their lives a little easier and maybe even more enjoyable. And who knows, I might even make some new friends.
What can I do to turn this scenario around?	• Educate myself. Do extensive research and get a good understanding of the illness, odds of survival, natural and medical remedies, potential options, and their pros and cons. This way, I'll be armed with knowledge when I speak with the medical practitioners and know what questions to ask. • Start a healthy lifestyle today. This means sleeping well, eating well, working out, and meditating every day, and making sure my environment is a positive, supportive, and optimistic one. This way, once I survive the battle (because I will!), I'll have already built good habits to reduce the risk of getting sick in the future. • Reach out to breast cancer groups to learn about others' experiences, so I can go into this with my eyes wide open, build a support community, and find ways to help others while I figure this out myself. And make some new friends while I'm at it!

Your Turn

This question may not apply to you right now.

If it does, write your biggest life challenge here. The simple act of writing a problem down will help you see it in a clearer light, so take a journal or write it down in the print copy of this book.

Here's Your First Step

My biggest life challenge:
_____

Now see if you can plug your answers to the Lemonade Maker questions in the table below. Seeing your answers on paper will give clarity to the problem and potential solutions.

The Lemonade Maker

Situation	What's keeping me up at night?	Is there a silver lining here?	What can I do to turn this scenario around?
#1			
#2			
#3			

FREE AUDIO DOWNLOAD

Get the shortcut to conquering your fears so you can follow your dreams. Learn as you go with the audio for this mini book.

Download your personal copy of the *Bust Your Fears* audio by clicking on the image or the link below.

Www.RebelDiva.Academy

I'll see you on the inside!

Tikiri

---

1. http://www.rebeldiva.academy/
2. http://www.rebelDiva.academy

BUST YOUR FEARS: 3 EASY TOOLS TO REDUCE YOUR STRESS & MAKE SMARTER CHOICES FASTER

"Fear, to a great extent, is born of a story we tell ourselves, and so I chose to tell myself a different story from the one women are told. I decided I was safe. I was strong. I was brave. Nothing could vanquish me. Insisting on this story was a form of mind control, but for the most part, it worked."
Cheryl Strayed

Have you picked up the other Rebel Divas workbooks?

The Rebel Diva Books

The Rebel Diva books are practical guides to finding your own personal power.

They incorporate lessons from the best self-help and personal development resources available today and synthesize them into simple guided exercises that anyone can use without drowning in detail. It took me more than a decade to learn the insights in here and create the tools in this series.

The questions in these books are simple, but their reach is deep. They're designed to make you contemplate your past, present, and future, and empower you to become a visionary for your own life. All the answers are in you. All these workbooks do is extract them one gentle question at a time and make you write them down, so you can start taking the first steps toward your future.

These books are not meant to sit and look pretty on a bookshelf but to be marked up, highlighted, and dog-eared with your scribbling all over the pages. Keep them on your bedside table with a pen, so you can reach them whenever you need a jolt of inspiration or want to track your progress.

Taking the time to find your life's purpose is time well spent.

For more, go to www.RebelDivas.com[3]

---

3. http://www.RebelDivas.com

Rebel Diva Book 1 - Your Rebel Dreams

This book will show you how to find the amazing things you're meant to do.

You'll discover your ultimate passions and purpose in life. You will go through a series of exercises including thirty-four questions on self-awareness to help you create a vision that matches your fundamental values, your innate desires, and your unique personality.

Rebel Diva Book 2 - Your Rebel Plans

This book will show you how to make your dreams come alive.

You will go through a series of easy-to-follow personalized exercises derived from more sophisticated management models. They will help you identify your core goals and create an action plan for your life. You'll also learn how to track your progress along the way. At the end of this workbook, you'll have a treasure map to get to your life dreams, a map that will help you stay on your game, no matter what.

Rebel Diva Book 3 - Your Rebel Life

This book will give you one hundred life tips for the ten most important pillars of your life. These are the facets of your life you need to pay special attention to if you want to be happy and fulfilled. You'll learn how to design a healthy, harmonious, and holistic lifestyle that's in tune with the fundamental values you identified in *Your Rebel Dreams* and the ambitions you wrote down in *Your Rebel Plans*.

About the Author

Tikiri Herath is the multiple-award-winning Canadian author of the Red Heeled Rebels international thriller novels.

Born on a tropical island in the Indian Ocean, she grew up in Southern Africa, and has lived and worked in Southeast Asia, Europe, and North America.

Starting as a lone immigrant girl with $20 in her pocket, she went on to receive a Bachelor's degree from the University of Victoria, British Columbia and a Master's degree from the Solvay Business School in Brussels, Belgium. For fifteen years, she worked in risk management in the intelligence and defense sectors, including the Canadian Federal Government and at NATO.

Tikiri's an adrenaline junkie who has rock climbed, bungee jumped, rode on the back of a motorcycle across Quebec, flown in an acrobatic airplane upside down, and parachuted solo.

But when she's not writing or plotting another thriller scene, you'll most probably find her baking in her kitchen with a glass of red wine in hand and jazz playing in the background.

To say hello, go to www.TikiriHerath.com[4].

---

4. http://www.TikiriHerath.com

Acknowledgments and many thanks go to Flavia Leung for giving this booklet a look through her professional risk management lens.

Copyright

All rights reserved. The use of any part of this publication, reproduced, transmitted in any form or by any means electronic, mechanical, photocopying, recording, or otherwise or stored in a retrieval system without prior written consent of the publisher—or in the case of photocopying or other reprographic copying, a license from the Canadian Copyright Licensing Agency—is an infringement of the copyright law.

The advice and strategies contained here may not be suitable or applicable to everyone or to every situation. Reading this work does not construe an engagement between the author/publisher and the reader, and the author/publisher is not rendering any legal, psychological, accounting or any other professional services through this work. Neither the author nor the publisher will be liable for damages arising from here.

The books and website links cited here are only for information and educational purposes and does not mean the author or the publisher endorses everything provided via these external resources. While the author will make every effort to ensure the links in this book remain updated, there is no guarantee the external sites may always be available or provide what they had initially.

Copyright ©2019 Tikiri Herath
Edition: 2019
Library & Archives Canada Cataloging in Publication
ISBN: 978-1-7751956-4-1[5]
Author: Tikiri Herath
Editor: Stephanie Parent
Publisher: The Rebel Diva Academy®
www.RebelDivas.com

---

5. https://www.collectionscanada.gc.ca/ciss-ssci/app/index.php?fuseaction=logbook.edit&publication=568216&lang=eng

www.RebelDivas.com

Don't miss out!

Visit the website below and you can sign up to receive emails whenever Tikiri Herath publishes a new book. There's no charge and no obligation.

https://books2read.com/r/B-A-QRFF-SRPW

BOOKS 2 READ

Connecting independent readers to independent writers.

www.ingramcontent.com/pod-product-compliance
Lightning Source LLC
Chambersburg PA
CBHW062200100526
44589CB00014B/1890